Scales & Modes

of

World Music

by Todd Milne

A Scale-Mode-Chord Matrix
Containing 252 Musical Scales
Illustrating Structure, Relationships and Applications
Includes Chord Harmonization and an Index of Traditional Names

FOR ALL INSTRUMENTS ~ INCLUDES GUITAR FRETBOARD MAPS

SCALES & MODES OF WORLD MUSIC

~ CONTENTS ~

How Many Scales & Modes Are There?

Scales are the basis of melodic structure in music. In the 12-tone system, there are 2051 different ways to traverse the octave, including crawling up the twelve tones of the chromatic scale one at a time, a simple octave leap, or all the different ways that we could arrange 2, 3, 4, 5, 6, 7, 8, 9, 10, or 11 tones. But how many of these could really be considered scales? What is a scale? Most of the scales used in western music are formed purely of half-steps and whole-steps. But others, including many from cultures around the world, contain larger and more varied scale steps. Even though most musics of the worlds cultures do not use the 12-tone *equal tempered* scale as their basis, the difference in the notes used is generally in small degrees of pitch variation (more info on pages 19-20), and the basic structure of these scales can still be roughly expressed in a 12-tone system. The vast majority of traditional scales used throughout the world contain seven notes. Use of 7 tones provides a complete scale structure without excessive chromatic runs that obscure melodic character, but patterns consisting of 5, 6, 8, 9 or 10 tones could definitely be considered scales. I list a few of them in the CHORD-SCALE MATRIX OF WESTERN HARMONY (page 14) and the INDEX OF TRADITIONAL SCALE NAMES (pages 18-19).

What Does the Scale-Mode-Chord Matrix Show?

The Matrix Contains 4 Layers of Information:

1) Scales - interval recipes for 252 unique musical scales
2) Steps - graphic illustration of the step pattern of each scale
3) Modes - graphic illustration of the modal relationships between the scales
4) Chords - all available diatonic chord tones for each step of every scale

I have been a collector of scales for quite a number of years, finding in each pattern new musical ideas for composition and improvisation. In this work I wanted to include all these scales & modes in the most concise way possible, showing their relationships to one another, and demonstrating some common ground between the musics of the world. I believe the Scale-Mode-Chord Matrix is the most complete resource for scales, their modes, and the available chords within each structure.

HOW TO USE THE MATRIX

Intervals - We begin with intervals, the basic building blocks of scales. Intervals are not specific tones like the note C, but rather the distance between notes. For example, the pairs of notes C-D, E-F#, and A-B are each two half-steps apart (a.k.a. a whole-step or Major 2nd), even though they are sounded at different pitches:

C	C#	D	D#	E	F	F#	G	G#	A	A#	B	C

two half-steps · · · two half-steps · · · two half-steps

All scales are based on a tonic note, represented by the number 1 *(for this reason, I do not show "1" for each scale in the matrix, as it is assumed in all cases)*. In our 12-tone system, the other 11 intervals can have a variety of names depending on the musical situation. For instance, the interval I have labeled "T" - a Tritone, could also be referred to as a raised 4th or lowered 5th. *For consistency throughout the matrix, I represent the twelve intervals of the chromatic scale as follows:*

$$1 \sim m2 \sim 2 \sim m3 \sim 3 \sim 4 \sim T \sim 5 \sim m6 \sim 6 \sim m7 \sim 7 \sim 1$$
memorize this row of numbers

These would be spoken: Tonic, minor 2nd, Major 2nd, minor 3rd, Major 3rd, Perfect 4th, Tritone, Perfect 5th, minor 6th, Major 6th, minor 7th, Major 7th, Tonic or Octave. This is the basis of everything else contained here. *Each row in the matrix is an illustration of the 12 chromatic tones in an octave.*

Scales - The simplest way to visualize a scale is as a series of notes ascending in a (more-or-less) step-wise fashion, beginning on a defined tonic note and ending with that same tone one octave higher. In actual music, the melody can of course wiggle, jump and otherwise use the notes of the scale in any number of ways, but we see the structure most clearly by arranging the notes in a straight line.

All scales are defined by their particular set of interval ingredients. For example, the scales C Major (C-D-E-F-G-A-B-C) and E Major (E-F#-G#-A-B-C#-D#-E) are the "Major" scales in the keys of "C" and "E" (i.e. they are based on different tonic notes). Even though they are different sets of tones, they are both "Major" scales because the notes of the two groups have the same relationships (2-3-4-5-6-7) to their respective tonics:

Major Scale	1	m2	2	m3	3	4	T	5	m6	6	m7	7	1
C Major Scale	C	C#	D	D#	E	F	F#	G	G#	A	A#	B	C
E Major Scale	E		F#	G	G#	A	A#	B	C	C#	D	D#	E

In the matrix, each box represents a separate, unique scale. The numbers in the box are the interval ingredients of that scale. The shaded scales have traditional names. Those shaded in black are the Primary Regular Scales. The outlined scale boxes designate the 48 regular scales. The blank boxes are tones not used in the scale. Here is the first row of the REGULAR SCALE MATRIX:

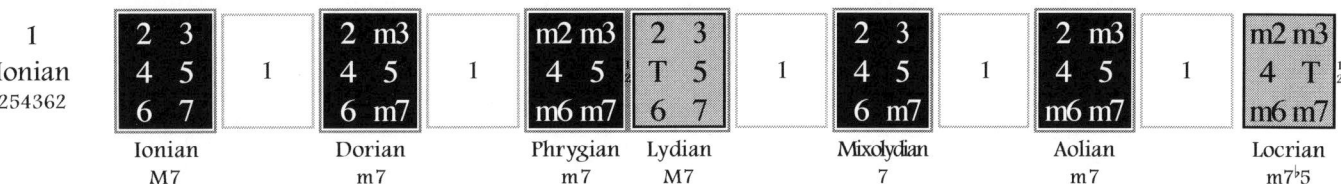

1							
Ionian 254362	Ionian M7	Dorian m7	Phrygian m7	Lydian M7	Mixolydian 7	Aolian m7	Locrian m7♭5

Steps - Every scale can also be defined by the unique pattern of steps from one tone to the next, beginning from the tonic. *The boxes in the matrix are arranged to show the step-size patterns. Two scale tones (the boxes with numbers) adjacent to each other are a half-step apart, just like two keys on a piano or two frets on a guitar. The blank boxes are tones not used in the scale. As indicated: 1 blank box between two scale tones represents a whole step , 2 blanks = a step-and-a-half, 3 blanks = two whole steps, etc.*

Modes - If we take any scale and start on a tone *other than* the tonic, and climb up through the notes of that scale, and end on the same tone one octave higher, we are playing a mode of that scale. Every scale has modes based on each tone of the scale - each a scale unto itself. The term mode is used to describe the relationship between scales that share the same tones but start on different notes. *The arrangement of the boxes in the matrix also illustrates the modal relationships between the scales.*

Groups - A scale and all its modal relatives is referred to as a group. *Each row in the matrix is a separate group, so that all scales in a single row are modes of each other. The groups are numbered down the left margin of each page.*

Interval Inventory - *Under the name of each group is a 6 digit number that designates the interval inventory of that group. The 6 digits represent the number of m2s, 2s, m3s, 3s, 4s & Ts respectively.* The other 5 intervals need not be listed separately as they are inversions of these and therefore occur the same amount of times in the particular group. The Tritone is an inversion of itself.

Locating Scales in the Matrix - *In the matrix, each scale can be located using two numbers to designate: a) it's group, and b) a number to indicate which mode it is in that group (count the scales starting from the left). The Major Scale would then be designated by the numbers 1 / 1. Meaning that it is in the first group (row) of scales, and it is the 1st scale over from the left in that group. Most of the Scales are located on the REGULAR SCALE MATRIX (pages 6~9). I use a superscript [I] and [W] to indicate the IRREGULAR SCALE MATRIX (pages 10-13) and the MATRIX OF WESTERN HARMONY (page 14) respectively.* I use this number designation in the tables of TRADITIONAL SCALES OF THE WORLD (pages 4-5) and the INDEX OF TRADITIONAL SCALE NAMES (pages 18-19) to connect all the scales listed there with their positions in the matrix.

INSTRUMENTS - The Major scale is the basis of how the intervals are named. If you have done any previous work with scales, you probably started with the Major scale. If you know the Major scale in all twelve keys on your instrument, or even one key, then all the other scales can be visualized as alterations of this starting point. On many instruments it is easy to visualize the twelve half-steps in the octave, so that looking at the matrix is pretty much like having a picture drawn of where the notes fall on the instrument. On the piano the notes are very obviously one right after the other. String instruments add the complication of multiple strings tuned to different notes. *The matrix pages include guitar fretboard maps of the first scale in each group. The other modes of the group use the same fretboard pattern starting on their respective scale degrees. These are slide rule type guides where the tonic note (1) aligns to the tonic note of the scale you want to play (A, C♯, B♭, etc.). These maps show the locations of the chord tones as they are repeated all over the neck of the guitar.* Here are full interval maps for guitar and other common string instruments:

Interval Layout for Guitar (Standard Tuning)

5	m6	6	m7	7	1	m2	2	m3	3	4	T	5	m6	6	m7	7	1
2	m3	3	4	T	5	m6	6	m7	7	1	m2	2	m3	3	4	T	5
m7	7	1	m2	2	m3	3	4	T	5	m6	6	m7	7	1	m2	2	m3
4	T	5	m6	6	m7	7	1	m2	2	m3	3	4	T	5	m6	6	m7
1	m2	2	m3	3	4	T	5	m6	6	m7	7	1	m2	2	m3	3	4
5	m6	6	m7	7	1	m2	2	m3	3	4	T	5	m6	6	m7	7	1

Interval Layout for Mandolin, Violin, Viola, Cello... (Strings tuned in 5ths)

3	4	T	5	m6	6	m7	7	1	m2	2	m3	3	4	T	5	m6	6
6	m7	7	1	m2	2	m3	3	4	T	5	m6	6	m7	7	1	m2	2
2	m3	3	4	T	5	m6	6	m7	7	1	m2	2	m3	3	4	T	5
5	m6	6	m7	7	1	m2	2	m3	3	4	T	5	m6	6	m7	7	1

THE SCALES & MODES OF WORLD MUSIC

Tetrachords/Pentachords - Tetrachords are not chords at all, but rather scale fragments spanning the interval of a perfect 4th rather than an octave. Raised 4ths would be indicated by a pentachord: a scale fragment spanning the interval of a perfect 5th. The most often used scales in music throughout the world contain a perfect 5th interval, and can therefore be described as a combination of a lower tetrachord (or pentachord) and an upper tetrachord. The lower tetrachord (root-2nd-3rd-4th) or pentachord (root-2nd-3rd-Tritone-5th) defines the quality of the 2nd & 3rd scale tones, while the upper tetrachord (5th-6th-7th-octave) defines the quality of the 6th & 7th scale tones. All of these scale tones may be major or minor. Most traditional scales can be defined by 4 Regular Tetrachords:

Tetrachord Steps	Lower Tetrachord (Pentachord)	Upper Tetrachord
whole/whole/half	1-2-3-4 (1-2-3-T-5)	5-6-7-8 (octave)
whole/half/whole	1-2-m3-4 (1-2-m3-T-5)	5-6-m7-8 (octave)
half/whole/whole	1-m2-m3-4 (1-m2-m3-T-5)	5-m6-m7-8 (octave)
half/step-and-a-half/half	1-m2-3-4 (1-m2-3-T-5)	5-m6-7-8 (octave)

Combining the 4 Regular Tetrachords in upper and lower positions give us the 16 Primary Regular Scales (4x4=16). The combinations containing the 4 regular pentachords (lower position) with the 4 regular tetrachords (upper position) give us the 16 Secondary Regular Scales (4x4=16).

Many cultures of the world recognize tetrachords as a basis for organizing scales. Tetrachords are especially prominent in the Maqam system of Middle Eastern Classical Music, where they are used as the foundation of melodic structure and modulation. Middle Eastern music is distinct in it's use of "quarter-tones" or "half-flats" so the possible tetrachords are more numerous. I'll not go into these here as the theory of quarter-tones would indicate a 24-tone system, although I do list some quarter tone scales on page 19.

The South Indian Melekartha system contains 72 parent scales or Melas. These scales all contain a perfect 5th, with the upper and lower tetrachords corresponding to the regular tetrachords mentioned above plus 2 irregular tetrachords: (half/half/step-and-a-half) and (step-and-a-half/half/half). Since this now includes 6 basic tetrachords to choose from for the lower and upper positions of the scale, we end up with 36 (6x6) different patterns. Add to this all these same scales with a raised 4th, and you arrive at the 72 (36x2) Melas. It just so happens that all basic 12-tone scale forms throughout the world end up corresponding to one of these Melas or is a mode thereof. This being the case, I decided to use these as the foundation of this work. The tables on the next 2 pages contain the 32 Regular and 40 Irregular Scales. The regular scales use only the 4 regular tetrachords/pentachords, while the irregular scales contain at least one irregular tetrachord/pentachord.

Name Origins - I have designated the South Indian names with a superscript [NUMBER] to indicate it's position in the original Melekartha system. Modern Western names are unmarked. A superscript [E]=Old Europe, [H]=Hebrew, [M]=Middle Eastern, [I]=North Indian, [J]=Japanese & [X]=Common Slang.

IN THE MATRIX - The 16 groups shown in the REGULAR SCALE MATRIX (pages 6-9) contain all the Regular Scales plus a large portion of the Irregular Scales as modal relatives. The Regular Scales are indicated by outlined boxes, with the 16 Primary Regular Scales shaded black. All other traditional scales are shaded grey. The scales of this matrix also include a shorthand designation based on the 7 modes of the Major Scale group. The remainder of the Irregular Scales are contained within the 20 groups shown in the IRREGULAR SCALE MATRIX (pages 10-13). The CHORD-SCALE MATRIX OF WESTERN HARMONY (page 14) lists the primary scales of Jazz, Blues & European Classical music, including the most prominent non-7-tone scales. All three matrixes list foundational chord forms for each scale, outlining the basic modal harmony.

TRADITIONAL SCALES OF THE WORLD

PRIMARY REGULAR SCALES (4~5)

1	2	3	4	5	6	7	Mode		Names
1	2	3	4	5	6	7	Ionian	1/1	Major, Ionian[E], Ajam[M], Bilaval[I], Dhirashankarabharanam[29]
1	2	m3	4	5	6	7	Ion♭3	2/1	Melodic Minor, Hawaiian, Esfahan[M], Gowrimanohari[23]
1	m2	m3	4	5	6	7	Ion♭2♭3	3/1	Neapolitan, Kokilapriya[11]
1	m2	3	4	5	6	7	Ion♭2	4/1	Suryakantam[17]
1	2	3	4	5	6	m7	Mixolydian	1/5	Mixolydian[E], Afshari[M], Chahargah, Kammaj[I], Harikambhoji[28]
1	2	m3	4	5	6	m7	Dorian	1/2	Dorian[E], Nava[M], Kafi[I], Karaharapriya[22], Ritsu[J]
1	m2	m3	4	5	6	m7	Dor♭2	2/2	Javanese[X], Natakapriya[10]
1	m2	3	4	5	6	m7	Mix♭2	5/5	Zanjaran[M], Ahir Bhairav[I], Chakravakam[16]
1	2	3	4	5	m6	m7	Mix♭6	2/5	Melodic Major, Hindu[X], Homayun[M], Charukeshi[26]
1	2	m3	4	5	m6	m7	Aolian	1/6	Natural Minor, Aolian[E], Nahawand (descending)[M], Asvari[I], Natabhairavi[20]
1	m2	m3	4	5	m6	m7	Phrygian	1/3	Phrygian[E], Kurd[M], Bhairavi[I], Hanumathodi[8], In[J]
1	m2	3	4	5	m6	m7	Phr#3	6/5	Phrygian Dominant, Spanish[X], Ahaba Rabba[H], Hijaz[M], Vakulabharanam[14]
1	2	3	4	5	m6	7	Ion♭6	5/1	Harmonic Major, Shawq Afza[M], Nat Bhairava[I], Sarasangi[27]
1	2	m3	4	5	m6	7	Aol#7	6/1	Harmonic Minor, Mohammedan[X], Nahawand (ascending)[M], Kiravani[21]
1	m2	m3	4	5	m6	7	Phr#7	7/1	Neapolitan Minor, Dhenuka[9]
1	m2	3	4	5	m6	7	Ion♭2♭6	8/1	Double Harmonic, Byzantine[X], Hijaz Kar[M], Bhairava[I], Mayamalava Gowla[15]

SECONDARY REGULAR SCALES (T~5)

1	2	3	T	5	6	7	Mode		Names
1	2	3	T	5	6	7	Lydian	1/4	Lydian[E], Kalyan[I], Mechakalyani[65], Ryo[J]
1	2	m3	T	5	6	7	Lyd♭3	5/4	Dharmavathi[59]
1	m2	m3	T	5	6	7	Lyd♭2♭3	9/1	Suvarnagi[47]
1	m2	3	T	5	6	7	Lyd♭2	13/1	Marava[I], Gamanashrama[53]
1	2	3	T	5	6	m7	Lyd♭7	2/4	Lydian Dominant, Vachaspathi[64]
1	2	m3	T	5	6	m7	Dor#4	6/4	Romanian[X], Tunisian[X], Nakriz[M], Hemavathi[58]
1	m2	m3	T	5	6	m7	Phr#4#6	10/1	Shadhuidha Margini[46]
1	m2	3	T	5	6	m7	Lyd♭2♭7	14/1	Ramapriya[52]
1	2	3	T	5	m6	m7	Lyd♭6♭7	3/4	Lydian Minor, Rishabhapriya[62]
1	2	m3	T	5	m6	m7	Aol#4	7/4	Hungarian Gypsy[X], Shanmukapriya[56]
1	m2	m3	T	5	m6	m7	Phr#4	11/1	Bhavapriya[44]
1	m2	3	T	5	m6	m7	Phr#3#4	15/1	Namanarayani[50]
1	2	3	T	5	m6	7	Lyd♭6	4/4	Lathangi[63]
1	2	m3	T	5	m6	7	Lyd♭3♭6	8/4	Gypsy Minor[X], Hungarian Minor[X], Nawa Athar[M], Simhendra Madhyamam[57]
1	m2	m3	T	5	m6	7	Phr#4#7	12/1	Athar Kurd[M], Todi[I], Shubhapanthuvarali[45]
1	m2	3	T	5	m6	7	Lyd♭2♭6	16/1	Pooravi[I], Kamanvardhini[51]

ADDITIONAL SCALES IN THE MATRIX

Arabian[X] (2~3~4~T~m6~m7) 3/5

Enigmatic (m2~3~T~m6~m7~7) [I]3/2

Leading Whole Tone (2~3~T~m6~m7~7) 3/2

Locrian[E] (m2~m3~4~T~m6~m7) 1/7

Lydian Augmented (2~3~T~m6~6~7) 2/3

Major Locrian (2~3~4~T~m6~m7) 3/5

Nahawand Murassah[M] (2~m3~4~T~6~m7) 5/2

Nohkan[J] (2~4~T~m6~6~7) 10/2

Oriental[X] (m2~3~4~T~6~m7) 8/5

Persian[X] (m2~3~4~T~m6~7) 12/5

Super Locrian (m2~m3~3~T~m6~m7) 2/7

Zamzam[M] (m2~m3~3~5~m6~m7) 5/3

1							Mode	Ratio	Name
1	2	3	4	5	m7	7	Ion#6	11/6	Naganandhini[30]
1	2	m3	4	5	m7	7	Ion♭3#6	^{1}8/1	Varunapriya[24]
1	m2	m3	4	5	m7	7	Ion♭2♭3#6	^{1}5/1	Rupavathi[12]
1	m2	3	4	5	m7	7	Ion♭2#6	^{1}13/1	Hatakambari[18]
1	m3	3	4	5	m7	7	Ion#2#6	12/6	Chalanata[36]
1	m2	2	4	5	m7	7	Ion♭2♭3#6	^{1}4/1	Thanarupi[6]
1	2	3	4	5	m6	6	Mix♭6♭7	^{1}2/4	Mararanjani[25]
1	2	m3	4	5	m6	6	Aol♭7	13/3	Jankaradhvani[19]
1	m2	m3	4	5	m6	6	Phry♭7	4/3	Senavathi[7]
1	m2	3	4	5	m6	6	Phry#3♭7	^{1}6/1	Gayakapriya[13]
1	m3	3	4	5	m6	6	Mix#2♭6♭7	^{1}9/1	Yagapriya[31]
1	m2	2	4	5	m6	6	Phr♭3♭7	16/7	Kanakangi[1]
1	m3	3	4	5	6	7	Ion#2	7/6	Shulini[35]
1	m3	3	4	5	6	m7	Mix#2	11/3	Vagadhisvari[34]
1	m3	3	4	5	m6	m7	Mix#2♭6	^{1}8/5	Ragavardhani[32]
1	m3	3	4	5	m6	7	Ion#2♭6	^{1}10/1	Gangeyabhushani[33]
1	m2	2	4	5	6	7	Ion♭2♭3	^{1}3/1	Manavathi[5]
1	m2	2	4	5	6	m7	Dor♭2♭3	^{1}2/1	Vanaspathi[4]
1	m2	2	4	5	m6	m7	Phry♭3	13/7	Rathnagi[2]
1	m2	2	4	5	m6	7	Phry♭3#7	^{1}1/1	Ganamurthi[3]

1							Mode	Ratio	Name
1	2	3	T	5	m7	7	Lyd#6	7/2	Chithrambari[66]
1	2	m3	T	5	m7	7	Lyd♭3#6	^{1}10/4	Nithimathi[60]
1	m2	m3	T	5	m7	7	Lyd♭2♭3#6	^{1}17/1	Enigmatic Minor, Dhivyamani[48]
1	m2	3	T	5	m7	7	Lyd♭2#6	^{1}1/2	Vishvambhari[54]
1	m3	3	T	5	m7	7	Lyd#2#6	8/2	Rasikapriya[72]
1	m2	2	T	5	m7	7	Lyd♭2♭3#6	^{1}16/1	Ragupriya[42]
1	2	3	T	5	m6	6	Lyd♭6♭7	^{1}3/4	Kanthamani[61]
1	2	m3	T	5	m6	6	Aol#4♭7	^{1}1/4	Shyamalangi[55]
1	m2	m3	T	5	m6	6	Phry#4♭7	^{1}7/3	Gavambodhi[43]
1	m2	3	T	5	m6	6	Phry#3#4♭7	^{1}18/1	Dhavalambari[49]
1	m3	3	T	5	m6	6	Lyd#2♭6♭7	^{1}19/1	Sucharithra[67]
1	m2	2	T	5	m6	6	Phr♭3#4♭7	^{1}11/1	Salagam[37]
1	m3	3	T	5	6	7	Lyd#2	6/6	Kosalam[71]
1	m3	3	T	5	6	m7	Lyd#2♭7	10/3	Hungarian Major[X], Nasika Bhushani[70]
1	m3	3	T	5	m6	m7	Lyd#2♭6♭7	^{1}20/1	Jyothsvarupini[68]
1	m3	3	T	5	m6	7	Lyd#2♭6	^{1}6/2	Dhatuvardhani[69]
1	m2	2	T	5	6	7	Lyd♭2♭3	^{1}15/1	Pavani[41]
1	m2	2	T	5	6	m7	Dor♭2♭3#4	^{1}14/1	Navanitham[40]
1	m2	2	T	5	m6	m7	Phry♭3#4	^{1}12/1	Jalarnavam[38]
1	m2	2	T	5	m6	7	Phry♭3#4#7	^{1}13/1	Jalavarali[39]

PRIMARY REGULAR SCALE MATRIX
Including the 16 Primary (4-5) Regular Scales + 8 Secondary (T-5) and 8 Third Order (4-T) Regular Scales

1 — Major — 254362

2 3 / 4 5 / 6 7	1	2 m3 / 4 5 / 6 m7	1	m2 m3 / 4 5 / m6 m7	2 3 / T 5 / 6 7	1	2 3 / 4 5 / 6 m7	1	2 m3 / 4 5 / m6 m7	1	m2 m3 / 4 T / m6 m7

Ionian M7 · Dorian m7 · Phrygian m7 · Lydian M7 · Mixolydian 7 · Aolian m7 · Locrian m7♭5

2 — Melodic Minor — 254444

Ion♭3 m^M7 · Dor♭2 m7 · Lyd♯5 +^M7 · Lyd♭7 7 · Mix♭6 7 · Aol♭5 m7♭5 · Loc♭4 m7♭5 7♭5/+7

3 — Neapolitan — 262626

Ion♭2♭3 m^M7 · Lyd♯5♯6 +^M7 7♭5/+7 · Mix♯4♯5 +7 7♭5 · Lyd♭6♭7 7 · Mix♭5♭6 7♭5 +7 · Aol♭4♭5 m7♭5 7♭5/+7 · Loc♭3♭4 7♭5 +7

4 — Suryakantam — 343544

Ion♭2 M7 · Lyd♯2♯5♯6 +^M7/+7/7♭5 m7♭5/m^M7♭5 · Phr♭7 m6 · Lyd♭6 M7 · Mix♭5 7♭5 · Aol♭4 m7 7 · Loc♭3

5 — Harmonic Major — 335444

Ion♭6 M7 · Dor♭5 m7♭5 · Phr♭4 m7 7 · Lyd♭3 m^M7 · Mix♭2 7 · Lyd♯2♯5 +^M7 m7♭5 · Loc♭7 dim7

6 — Harmonic Minor — 335444

Aol♯7 m^M7 · Loc♯6 m7♭5 · Ion♯5 +^M7 · Dor♯4 m7 · Phr♯3 7 · Lyd♯2 M7 m^M7 · Loc♭4♭7 dim7

7 — Neapolitan Minor — 343544

Phr♯7 m^M7 · Lyd♯6 M7 7 · Mix♯5 +7 · Aol♯4 m7 · Loc♯3 7♭5 +7 · Ion♯2 M7 m^M7 · Loc♭3♭4♭7

8 — Double Harmonic — 424544

Ion♭2♭6 M7 · Lyd♯2♯6 M7/7 m7/m^M7 · Phr♭4♭7 m6 M6 · Lyd♭3♭6 m^M7 · Mix♭2♭5 7♭5 · Ion♯2♯5 +^M7 · Loc♭3♭7

PRIMARY REGULAR SCALE MATRIX ~ FRETBOARD MAPS
For Standard Tuning(1~4~m7~m3~5~1)

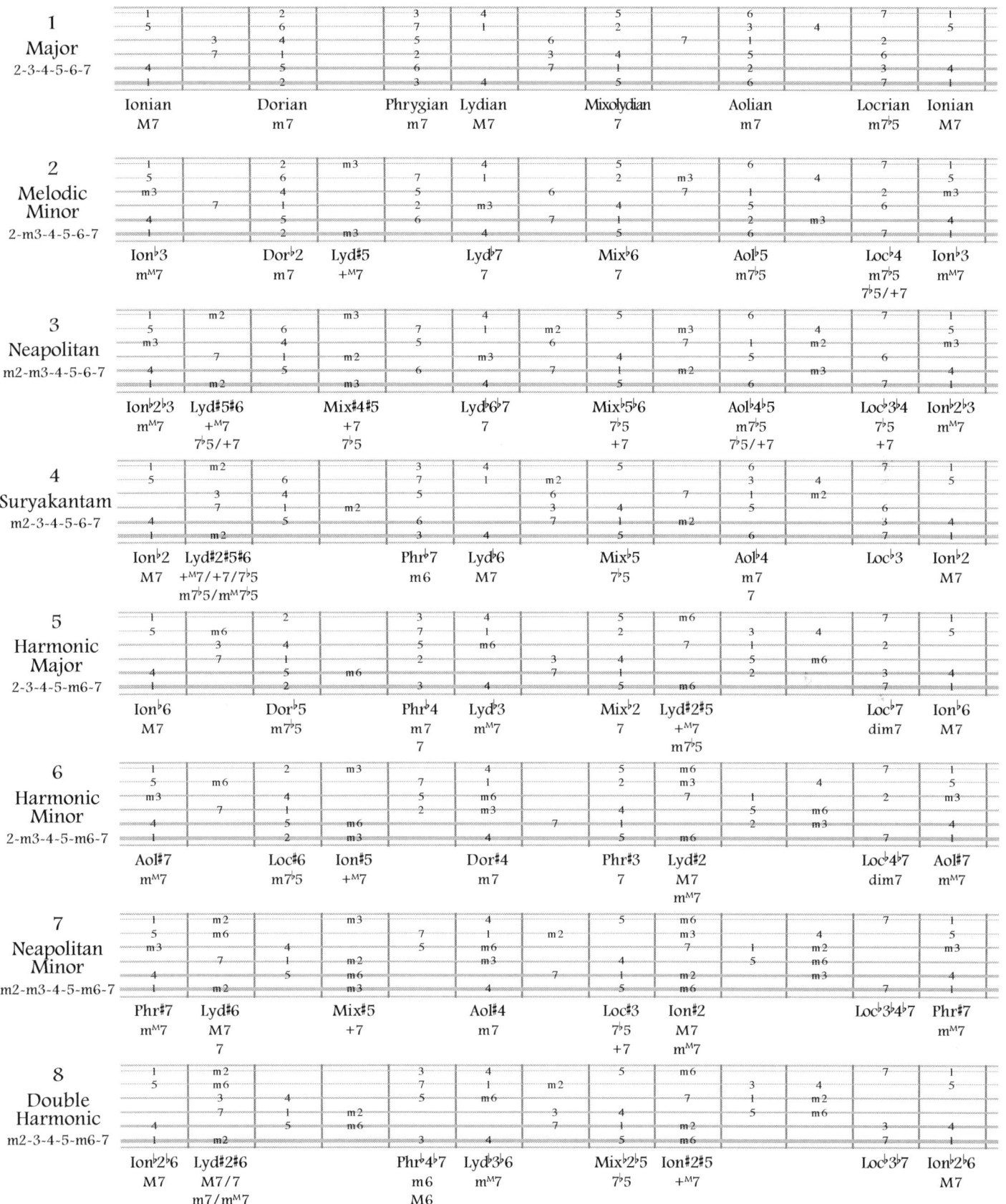

SECONDARY REGULAR SCALE MATRIX

Including the Remaining 8 Secondary (T~5) and 8 Third Order (4~T) Regular Scales

9 Suvarnagi 344436	m2 m3 T 5 6 7 ½ Lyd♭2♭3 m^{M}7	2 4 T m6 m7 7 Lyd♯3♯5♯6	1	m3 3 T m6 6 m7 Mix♯2♯4♯5 +7/7♭5 m7♭5	1½		m2 m3 4 T 5 6 ½ Loc♭6♭7 m6	2 3 4 T m6 7 Ion♭5♭6 +^{M}7	1	2 m3 3 T 6 m7 Dor♭4♭5 m7♭5 7♭5	1	m2 2 3 5 m6 m7 ½ Phr♭3♭4 7
10 Shadhuidha Margini 336336	m2 m3 T 5 6 m7 ½ Phr♯4♯6 m7	2 4 T m6 6 7 Lyd♯3♯5	1	m3 3 T 5 6 m7 Mix♯2♯4 7 m7	1½		m2 m3 3 T 5 6 ½ Loc♭4♭6♭7 M6	2 m3 4 T m6 7 Ion♭3♭5♭6 m^{M}7♭5	1	m2 m3 3 T 6 m7 ½ Dor♭2♭4♭5 m7♭5 7♭5	2 m3 4 m6 6 7 Dor♯5♯7 m^{M}7♯5	1
11 Bhavapriya 344354	m2 m3 T 5 m6 m7 ½ Phr♯4 m7	2 4 T 5 6 7 Lyd♯3 M7sus	1	m3 3 4 5 6 m7 Mix♯2 7 m7	1½		m2 2 3 T 5 6 ½ Loc♭3♭4♭6♭7 M6	m2 m3 4 T m6 7 ½ Loc♯7 m^{M}7♭5	2 3 4 5 m7 7 Ion♯6 M7 7	1	2 m3 4 m6 6 m7 Dor♯5 m7♯5	1
12 Todi 433454	m2 m3 T 5 m6 7 ½ Phr♯4♯7 m^{M}7	2 4 T 5 m7 7 Lyd♯3♯6 M7sus 7sus	1	m3 3 4 m6 6 m7 Mix♯2♯5 +7	1½		m2 2 4 T 5 6 ½ Loc♭3♭6♭7 6sus	m2 3 4 T m6 7 ½ Loc♯3♯7 +^{M}7	m3 3 4 5 m7 7 Ion♯2♯6 M7/7 m7/m^{M}7	1½		m2 2 3 5 m6 6 ½ Phr♭3♭4♭7 M6
13 Marava 344354	m2 3 T 5 6 7 ½ Lyd♭2 M7	m3 4 T m6 m7 7 Lyd♯2♯3♯5♯6 m7♭5 m^{M}7♭5	1½		2 m3 4 5 m6 6 Aol♭7 m6	1	m2 m3 4 T 5 m7 ½ Loc♭6 m7	2 3 4 T 6 7 Ion♭5 M7♭5	1	2 m3 3 5 6 m7 Dor♭4 m7 7	1	m2 2 4 5 m6 m7 ½ Phr♭3 7sus
14 Ramapriya 336336	m2 3 T 5 6 m7 ½ Lyd♭2♭7 7	m3 4 T m6 6 7 Lyd♯2♯3♯5 m^{M}7♭5	1½		2 m3 4 T m6 6 Aol♭5♭7 dim7	1	m2 m3 3 T 5 m7 ½ Loc♭4♭6 m7 7	2 m3 4 T 6 7 Ion♭3♭5 m^{M}7♭5	1	m2 m3 3 5 6 m7 ½ Dor♭2♭4 m7 7	2 m3 T m6 6 7 Lyd♭3♯5 m^{M}7♭5 dim7	1
15 Namanarayani 344436	m2 3 T 5 m6 m7 ½ Phr♯3♯4 7	m3 4 T 5 6 7 Lyd♯2♯3 m^{M}7	1½		2 m3 3 T m6 6 Aol♭4♭5♭7 dim7	1	m2 2 3 T 5 m7 ½ Loc♭3♭4♭6 7	m2 m3 4 T 6 7 ½ Loc♯6♯7 m^{M}7♭5	2 3 4 m6 m7 7 Ion♯5♯6 +^{M}7 +7	1	2 m3 T m6 6 m7 Dor♯4♯5 m7♭5	1
16 Pooravi 433454	m2 3 T 5 m6 7 ½ Lyd♭2♭6 M7	m3 4 T 5 m7 7 Lyd♯2♯3♯6 m^{M}7 m7	1½		2 m3 3 5 m6 6 Aol♭4♭7 m6 M6	1	m2 2 4 T 5 m7 ½ Loc♭3♭6 7sus	m2 3 4 T 6 7 ½ Ion♭2♭5 M7♭5	m3 3 4 m6 m7 7 Ion♯2♯5♯6 +^{M}7	1½		m2 2 4 5 m6 6 ½ Phr♭3♭7 6sus

SECONDARY REGULAR SCALE MATRIX ~ FRETBOARD MAPS
For Standard Tuning(1~4~m7~m3~5~1)

9 Suvarnagi
m2-m3-T-5-6-7

Lyd♭2♭3 — m^M7 | Lyd♯3♯5♯6 | Mix♯2♯4♯5 +7/7♭5 m7♭5 | Loc♭6♭7 m6 | Ion♭5♭6 +^M7 | Dor♭4♭5 m7♭5 7♭5 | Phr♭3♭4 7 | Lyd♭2♭3 m^M7

10 Shadhuidha Margini
m2-m3-T-5-6-m7

Phr♯4♯6 m7 | Lyd♯3♯5 | Mix♯2♯4 7 m7 | Loc♭4♭6♭7 M6 | Ion♭3♭5♭6 m^M7♭5 | Dor♭2♭4♭5 m7♭5 7♭5 | Dor♯5♯7 m^M7♯5 | Phr♯4♯6 m7

11 Bhavapriya
m2-m3-T-5-m6-m7

Phr♯4 m7 | Lyd♯3 M7sus | Mix♯2 7 m7 | Loc♭3♭4♭6♭7 M6 | Loc♯7 m^M7♭5 | Ion♯6 M7 7 | Dor♯5 m7♯5 | Phr♯4 m7

12 Todi
m2-m3-T-5-m6-7

Phr♯4♯7 m^M7 | Lyd♯3♯6 M7sus 7sus | Mix♯2♯5 +7 | Loc♭3♭6♭7 6sus | Loc♯3♯7 +^M7 | Ion♯2♯6 M7/7 m7/m^M7 | Phr♭3♭4♭7 M6 | Phr♯4♯7 m^M7

13 Marava
m2-3-T-5-6-7

Lyd♭2 M7 | Lyd♯2♯3♯5♯6 m7♭5 m^M7♭5 | Aol♭7 m6 | Loc♭6 m7 | Ion♭5 M7♭5 | Dor♭4 m7 7 | Phr♭3 7sus | Lyd♭2 M7

14 Ramapriya
m2-3-T-5-6-m7

Lyd♭2♭7 7 | Lyd♯2♯3♯5 m^M7♭5 | Aol♭5♭7 dim7 | Loc♭4♭6 m7 7 | Ion♭3♭5 m^M7♭5 | Dor♭2♭4 m7 7 | Lyd♭3♯5 m^M7♭5 dim7 | Lyd♭2♭7 7

15 Namanarayani
m2-3-T-5-m6-m7

Phr♯3♯4 7 | Lyd♭2♯3 m^M7 | Aol♯4♭5♭7 dim7 | Loc♭3♭4♭6 7 | Loc♯6♯7 m^M7♭5 | Ion♯5♯6 +^M7 +7 | Dor♯4♯5 m7♭5 | Phr♯3♯4 7

16 Pooravi
m2-3-T-5-m6-7

Lyd♭2♭6 M7 | Lyd♭2♯3♯6 m^M7 m7 | Aol♭4♭7 m6 M6 | Loc♭3♭6 7sus | Ion♭2♭6 M7♭5 | Ion♯2♯5♯6 +^M7 | Phr♭3♭7 6sus | Lyd♭2♭6 M7

Scales & Modes of World Music by Todd Milne ~ 9

PRIMARY IRREGULAR SCALE MATRIX

Including All Remaining Primary (4~5) Melakarthas

1 Ganamurthi 434346	m2 2 4 5 m6 7 ½	m2 3 T 5 m7 7 ½	m3 4 T 6 m7 7	1½		2 m3 T 5 m6 6	1	m2 3 4 T 5 m7 ½	m3 3 4 T 6 7	1½		m2 2 m3 T m6 6 ½
	M7sus	M7/7	m^{M}7♭5/m7♭5			m6		7	m^{M}7♭5			dim7
2 Vanaspathi 344452	m2 2 4 5 6 m7 ½	m2 3 T m6 6 7 ½	m3 4 5 m6 m7 7	1½		2 3 4 5 m6 6	1	2 m3 4 T 5 m7	1	m2 m3 3 4 m6 m7 ½	2 m3 3 5 6 7	1
	7sus	+^{M}7	m^{M}7/m7			M6		m7		+7	m^{M}7/M7	
3 Manavathi 353444	m2 2 4 5 6 7 ½	m2 3 T m6 m7 7 ½	m3 4 5 6 m7 7	1½		2 3 T 5 m6 6	1	2 3 4 T 5 m7	1	2 m3 3 4 m6 m7	1	m2 2 m3 T m6 m7 ½
	M7sus	+^{M}7/+7	m^{M}7/m7			M6		7		+7		m7♭5
4 Thanarupi 444344	m2 2 4 5 m7 7 ½	m2 3 T 6 m7 7 ½	m3 4 m6 6 m7 7	1½		2 4 T 5 m6 7	1	m3 3 4 T 5 m7	1½		m2 2 m3 3 5 6 ½	m2 2 m3 T 6 7 ½
	M7sus/7sus	7♭5	m^{M}7♯5/m7♯5			M7sus		7/m7			M6/m6	m^{M}7♭5
5 Rupavathi 353444	m2 m3 4 5 m7 7 ½	2 3 T 6 m7 7	1	2 3 5 m6 6 m7	1	2 4 T 5 m6 m7	1	m3 3 4 T m6 m7	1½		m2 2 m3 4 5 6 ½	m2 2 3 T m6 7 ½
	m^{M}7/m7	7♭5		7		7sus		7♭5/+7/m7♭5			m6	+^{M}7
6 Gayakapriya 424642	m2 3 4 5 m6 6 ½	m3 3 T 5 m6 7	1½		m2 m3 3 4 m6 6 ½	2 m3 3 5 m6 7	1	m2 2 4 T 6 m7 ½	m2 3 4 m6 6 7 ½	m3 3 5 m6 m7 7	1½	
	M6	M7/m^{M}7				m^{M}7/M7			+^{M}7	M7/m^{M}7 7/m7		
7 Hatakambari 434346	m2 3 4 5 m7 7 ½	m3 3 T 6 m7 7	1½		m2 m3 T 5 m6 6 ½	2 4 T 5 m6 7	1	m3 3 4 T 6 m7	1½		m2 2 m3 T 5 6 ½	m2 2 4 T m6 7 ½
	M7/7	m^{M}7♭5/m7♭5			m6	M7sus		7♭5/m7♭5			m6	
8 Varunapriya 344452	2 m3 4 5 m7 7	1	m2 m3 4 m6 6 m7 ½	2 3 5 m6 6 7	1	2 4 T 5 6 m7	1	m3 3 4 5 m6 m7	1½		m2 2 3 4 5 6 ½	m2 m3 3 T m6 7 ½
	m^{M}7/m7		m7♯5	M7		7sus		7/m7			M6	m^{M}7♭5/+^{M}7
9 Yagapriya 434542	m3 3 4 5 m6 6	1½		m2 2 3 4 T 6 ½	m2 m3 3 4 m6 7 ½	2 m3 3 5 m7 7	1	m2 2 4 m6 6 m7 ½	m2 3 5 m6 6 7 ½	m3 T 5 m6 m7 7	1½	
	M6/m6				+^{M}7	m^{M}7/m7 M7/7			M7	m^{M}7/m7		
10 Gangeyabhushani 424642	m3 3 4 5 m6 7	1½		m2 2 3 4 m6 6 ½	m2 m3 3 5 m6 7 ½	2 m3 T 5 m7 7	1	m2 3 4 m6 6 m7 ½	m3 3 5 m6 6 7	1½		m2 3 4 T m6 6 ½
	M7/m^{M}7				m^{M}7/M7	m^{M}7/m7		+7	M7/m^{M}7			

PRIMARY IRREGULAR SCALE MATRIX ~ FRETBOARD MAPS
For Standard Tuning(1~4~m7~m3~5~1)

1
Ganamurthi
m2-2-4-5-m6-7

M7sus   M7/7   m^M^7♭5/m7♭5   m6   7   m^M^7♭5   dim7   M7sus

2
Vanaspathi
m2-2-4-5-6-m7

7sus   +^M^7   m^M^7/m7   M6   m7   +7   m^M^7/M7   7sus

3
Manavathi
m2-2-4-5-6-7

M7sus   +^M^7/+7   m^M^7/m7   M6   7   +7   m7♭5   M7sus

4
Thanarupi
m2-2-4-5-m7-7

M7sus/7sus   7♭5   m^M^7♭5/m7♯5   M7sus   7/m7   M6/m6   m^M^7♭5   M7sus/7sus

5
Rupavathi
m2-m3-4-5-m7-7

m^M^7/m7   7♭5   7   7sus   7♭5/+7/m7♭5   m6   +^M^7   m^M^7/m7

6
Gayakapriya
m2-3-4-5-m6-6

M6   M7/m^M^7   m^M^7/M7   +^M^7   M7/m^M^7   7/m7   M6

7
Hatakambari
m2-3-4-5-m7-7

M7/7   m^M^7♭5   m7♭5   m6   M7sus   7♭5/m7♭5   m6   M7/7

8
Varunapriya
2-m3-4-5-m7-7

m^M^7/m7   m7♯5   M7   sus7   7/m7   M6   m^M^7♭5/+^M^7   m^M^7/m7

9
Yagapriya
m3-3-4-5-m6-6

M6/m6   +^M^7   m^M^7/m7/M7/7   M7   m^M^7/m7   M6/m6

10
Gangeyabhushani
m3-3-4-5-m6-7

M7/m^M^7   m^M^7/M7   m^M^7/m7   +7   M7/m^M^7   M7/m^M^7

SECONDARY IRREGULAR SCALE MATRIX

Including All Remaining Secondary (T~5) Melakarthas

11 Salagam 532356	m2 2 T 5 ½ m6 6 69	m2 4 T 5 ½ m6 7 M7sus4	3 4 T 5 m7 7 M7/7		2		m2 2 m3 T ½ 5 m6 m	m2 2 4 T ½ 5 7 M7sus	m2 3 4 T ½ m7 7 7♭5	m3 3 4 6 m7 7	1½	
12 Jalarnavam 442446	m2 2 T 5 ½ m6 m7 7sus2	m2 4 T 5 ½ 6 7 7sus4	3 4 T m6 m7 7 $+^{M}7$/+7		2		m2 2 3 T ½ 5 m6 M	m2 m3 4 T ½ 5 7 $m^{M}7$	2 3 4 T m7 7 7♭5	1	2 m3 3 m6 6 m7 +7	1
13 Jalavarali 532356	m2 2 T 5 ½ m6 7 M7sus2	m2 4 T 5 ½ m7 7 M7sus4/ 7sus4	3 4 T 6 m7 7 7♭5		2		m2 2 4 T ½ 5 m6 sus	m2 3 4 T ½ 5 7 M7	m3 3 4 T m7 7 7♭5/m7♭5 $m^{M}7$♭5	1½		m2 2 m3 5 ½ m6 6 m6
14 Navanitham 434444	m2 2 T 5 ½ 6 m7 7sus2	m2 4 T m6 ½ 6 7	3 4 5 m6 m7 7 M7/7		2		m2 m3 3 T ½ 5 m6 m/M	2 m3 4 T 5 7 $m^{M}7$	1	m2 m3 3 4 ½ 6 m7	2 m3 3 m6 6 7 $+^{M}7$	1
15 Pavani 443354	m2 2 T 5 ½ 6 7 M7sus2	m2 4 T m6 ½ m7 7	3 4 5 6 m7 7 M7/7		2		m2 m3 4 T ½ 5 m6 m	2 3 4 T 5 7 M7	1	2 m3 3 4 6 m7	1	m2 2 m3 5 ½ m6 m7 m7
16 Ragupriya 533444	m2 2 T 5 ½ m7 7 M7sus2/ 7sus2	m2 4 T 6 ½ m7 7	3 4 m6 6 m7 7 $+^{M}7$/+7		2		m2 3 4 T ½ 5 m6 M	m3 3 4 T 5 7 M7/$m^{M}7$	1½		m2 2 m3 3 ½ m6 6	m2 2 m3 5 ½ m6 7 $m^{M}7$
17 Dhivyamani 434444	m2 m3 T 5 ½ m7 7 $m^{M}7$/m7	2 4 T 6 m7 7	1	m3 3 5 m6 6 m7 7/m7	1½		m2 3 4 T ½ 5 6 M6	m3 3 4 T m6 7 $+^{M}7$/$m^{M}7$♭5	1½		m2 2 m3 4 ½ m6 6	m2 2 3 5 ½ m6 7 M7
18 Dhavalambari 434444	m2 3 T 5 ½ m6 6 M6	m3 4 T 5 m6 7 $m^{M}7$	1½		2 m3 3 4 m6 6 m6/M6	1	m2 2 m3 T ½ 5 m7 m7	m2 2 4 T ½ 6 7	m2 3 4 m6 ½ m7 7 $+^{M}7$/+7	m3 3 5 6 m7 7 M7/7 $m^{M}7$/m7	1½	
19 Sucharithra 435434	m3 3 T 5 m6 6 M6/m6	1½		m2 m3 3 4 ½ T 6 dim7	2 m3 3 4 m6 7 $+^{M}7$	1	m2 2 m3 T ½ 6 m7 m7♭5	m2 2 4 m6 ½ 6 7	m2 3 5 m6 ½ m7 7 M7/7	m3 T 5 6 m7 7 $m^{M}7$/m7	1½	
20 Jyothisvarupini 344534	m3 3 T 5 m6 m7 7/m7	1½		m2 m3 3 4 ½ 5 6 m6/M6	2 m3 3 T m6 7 $m^{M}7$♭5 $+^{M}7$	1	m2 2 3 T ½ 6 m7 7♭5	m2 m3 4 m6 ½ 6 7 m7♯5	2 3 5 m6 m7 7 M7/7	1	2 4 T m6 6 m7	1

SECONDARY IRREGULAR SCALE MATRIX ~ FRETBOARD MAPS
For Standard Tuning(1~4~m7~m3~5~1)

11 Salagam
m2-2-T-5-m6-6

69   M7sus4   M7/7   m   M7sus   7♭5   69

12 Jalarnavam
m2-2-T-5-m6-m7

7sus2   7sus4   +ᴹ7/+7   M   mᴹ7   7♭5   +7   7sus2

13 Jalavarali
m2-2-T-5-m6-7

M7sus2   M7sus4   7♭5   sus   M7   7♭5/mᵐ7♭5   m6   M7sus2
     7sus4   mᴹ7♭5

14 Navanitham
m2-2-T-5-6-m7

7sus2   M7/7   m/M   mᴹ7   +ᴹ7   7sus2

15 Pavani
m2-2-T-5-6-7

M7sus2   M7/7   m   M7   m7   M7sus2

16 Ragupriya
m2-2-T-5-m7-7

M7sus2   +ᴹ7/+7   M   M7/mᴹ7   mᴹ7   M7sus2
7sus2   7sus2

17 Dhivyamani
m2-m3-T-5-m7-7

mᴹ7/m7   7/m7   M6   +ᴹ7/mᴹ7♭5   M7   mᴹ7/m7

18 Dhavalambari
m2-3-T-5-m6-6

M6   mᴹ7   m6/M6   m7   +ᴹ7/+7   M7/7   M6
                                         mᴹ7/m7

19 Sucharithra
m3-3-T-5-m6-6

M6/m6   dim7   +ᴹ7   m7♭5   M7/7   mᴹ7/m7   M6/m6

20 Jyothisvarupini
m3-3-T-5-m6-m7

7/m7   m6/M6   mᴹ7♭5   7♭5   m7♯5   M7/7   7/m7
                   +ᴹ7

CHORD~SCALE MATRIX OF WESTERN HARMONY
Including the Primary Scales of Jazz, Blues & European Classical Music

1 Major/Minor 254444

2 3 / 4 5 / 6 7	1	2 m3 / 4 5 / 6 m7	1	m2 m3 / 4 5 ½ / m6 m7	2 3 / T 5 / 6 7	1	2 3 / 4 5 / 6 m7	1	2 m3 / 4 5 / m6 m7	1	m2 m3 / 4 T ½ / m6 m7

Major — M7 · Dorian — m7 · Phrygian — m7♭9♭13 · Lydian — M7♯11 · Mixolydian — 7 · Minor — m7♭13 · Locrian — m7♭5♭9♭13

2 Melodic Minor 254444

Melodic Minor — m^M7 · Dor♭2 — m7♭9 · Lydian Augmented — +^M7♯11 · Lydian Dominant — 7♯11 · Mix♭6 — 7♭13 · Aol♭5 — m7♭5♭13 · Super Locrian — 7♭5♭9♯9♭13

3 Harmonic Minor 335444

Harmonic Minor — m^M7♭13 · Loc♯6 — m7♭5♯9 · Ion♯5 — +^M7 · Dor♯4 — m7♯11 · Phrygian Dominant — 7♭9♭13 · Lyd♯2 — M7♯9♯11 · Loc♭4♭7 — dim7♭9♯11♭13

4 Diminished 448448

Diminished — dim7♭13 · Symetric Dominant — 7♭9♯9♯11 · Diminished · Symetric Dominant · Diminished · Symetric Dominant · Diminished · Symetric Dominant

5 Whole Tone 060606

2 3 / T m6 / m7	1	2 3 / T m6 / m7	1	2 3 / T m6 / m7	1	2 3 / T m6 / m7	1	2 3 / T m6 / m7	1	2 3 / T m6 / m7	1

Whole Tone — +7♯11(no13) · Whole Tone · Whole Tone · Whole Tone · Whole Tone · Whole Tone

6 Pentatonic 032140

2 3 / 5 6	1	2 4 / 5 m7	1	m3 4 / m6 m7	1½	2 4 / 5 6	1	m3 4 / 5 m7	1½

Pentatonic Major — M69 · Pentatonic Minor — m7add11

7 Blues 233242

2 m3 / 3 5 / 6	1	m2 2 / 4 5 / m7	m2 3 / T 6 / 7	m3 4 / m6 m7 / 7	1½	2 4 / 5 m6 / 6	1	m3 4 / T 5 / m7	1½

Blues Major · Blues Minor

CHORD HARMONIZATION

Chords can be defined in much the same way as scales. Each chord is characterized by a unique combination of intervals in relation to a tonic note. In some ways the only practical difference between a chord and a scale is that you play the notes of the chord simultaneously, while the notes of the scale are played in succession. Even when not the exact same combination of notes, it is by the common tones that we generally consider a scale and chord to be compatible. For instance, a Major scale (1-2-3-4-5-6-7) "goes with" a Major 7th chord (1-3-5-7), not a Minor 7th chord (1-m3-5-m7). *So to harmonize any scale in the matrix, Simply read the scale tones as available chord tones for each scale step. Additionally, I have listed possible foundational chords for the scales below each box.*

Below is a list of common chord types. Chord theory is generally based on stacked thirds, not steps like scales. So when you see 9, 11 & 13 in chord notation, we are referring to 2, 4 & 6 in the second octave:

Scale Intervals	1	m2	2	m3	3	4	T	5	m6	6	m7	7	1	m2	2	m3	3	4	T	5	m6	6
Upper Structure Chord Intervals													8	m9	9	m10	10	11	#11	12	m13	13

COMMON CHORD TYPES

3-note Chords (Triads)

M (1-3-5)
m (1-m3-5)
dim (1-m3-T$^{(b5)}$)
+ (1-3-m6$^{(#5)}$)
Sus4 (1-4-5)
Sus2 (1-2-5)

4-note Chords

M7 (1-3-5-7)
M6 (1-3-5-6)
m7 (1-m3-5-m7)
m6 (1-m3-5-6)
m^{M}7 (1-m3-5-7)
7 (1-3-5-m7)
7b5 (1-3-T$^{(b5)}$-m7)
7#5 (1-3-m6$^{(#5)}$-m7)
m7b5 (1-m3-T$^{(b5)}$-m7)

dim7 (1-m3-T$^{(b5)}$-6$^{(b7)}$)
+^{M}7 (1-3-m6$^{(#5)}$-m7)
7Sus4 (1-4-5-m7)
add9 (1-3-5-2$^{(9)}$)

5-note Chords

M9 (1-3-5-7-2$^{(9)}$)
m9 (1-m3-5-m7-2$^{(9)}$)
m7b9 (1-m3-5-m7-m2$^{(b9)}$)
m9^{M}7 (1-m3-5-7-2$^{(9)}$)
9 (1-3-5-m7-2$^{(9)}$)
9b5 (1-3-T$^{(b5)}$-m7-2$^{(9)}$)
9#5 (1-3-m6$^{(#5)}$-m7-2$^{(9)}$)
b9 (1-3-5-m7-m2$^{(b9)}$)
#9 (1-3-5-m7-m3$^{(#9)}$)
b9b5 (1-3-T$^{(b5)}$-m7-m2$^{(b9)}$)
6/9 (1-3-5-6-2$^{(9)}$)
m6/9 (1-m3-5-6-2$^{(9)}$)

9Sus4 (1-4-5-m7-2$^{(9)}$)

6-note Chords

M11 (1-3-5-7-2$^{(9)}$-4$^{(11)}$)
M#11 (1-3-5-7-2$^{(9)}$-T$^{(#11)}$)
m11 (1-m3-5-m7-2$^{(9)}$-4$^{(11)}$)
m11b9 (1-m3-5-m7-m2$^{(b9)}$-4$^{(11)}$)
11 (1-3-5-m7-2$^{(9)}$-4$^{(11)}$)
#11 (1-3-5-m7-2$^{(9)}$-T$^{(#11)}$)
+7#11 (1-3-m6$^{(#5)}$-m7-2$^{(9)}$-T$^{(#11)}$)
+^{M}7#11 (1-3-m6$^{(#5)}$-7-2$^{(9)}$-T$^{(#11)}$)
M13 (1-3-5-7-2$^{(9)}$-6$^{(13)}$)
m13 (1-m3-5-m7-2$^{(9)}$-6$^{(13)}$)
m7b13 (1-m3-5-m7-2$^{(9)}$-m6$^{(b13)}$)
m7b9b13 (1-m3-5-m7-m2$^{(b9)}$-m6$^{(b13)}$)
13 (1-3-5-m7-2$^{(9)}$-6$^{(13)}$)
13b9 (1-3-5-m7-m2$^{(b9)}$-6$^{(13)}$)
13b9b5 (1-3-T$^{(b5)}$-m7-m2$^{(b9)}$-6$^{(13)}$)

COMMON CHORD TYPES ~ FRETBOARD MAPS

The next two pages contain fretboard maps of the most common 3 and 4 note chords. These again are slide rule type guides where the tonic note (1) aligns to the tonic note of the chord you want to play (A, G#, Bb, etc.). These maps show the locations of the chord tones as they are repeated all over the neck of the guitar. The different chord voicings are created by choosing at least one of each chord tone to fill out the chord. Inversions are shown on the same map. In chord theory inversion is very similar the concept of mode in scale theory, and can be visualized the same way here. In general, inversions of a chord are not recognized as separate chords, but there are a few exceptions. For example: the sus2 chord (1-2-5) is the first inversion of the sus4 chord (1-4-5) on the next page, and is shown as having it's tonic on the "4" of the sus4.

COMMON CHORD TYPES ~ FRETBOARD MAPS
For Standard Tuning(1~4~m7~m3~5~1)

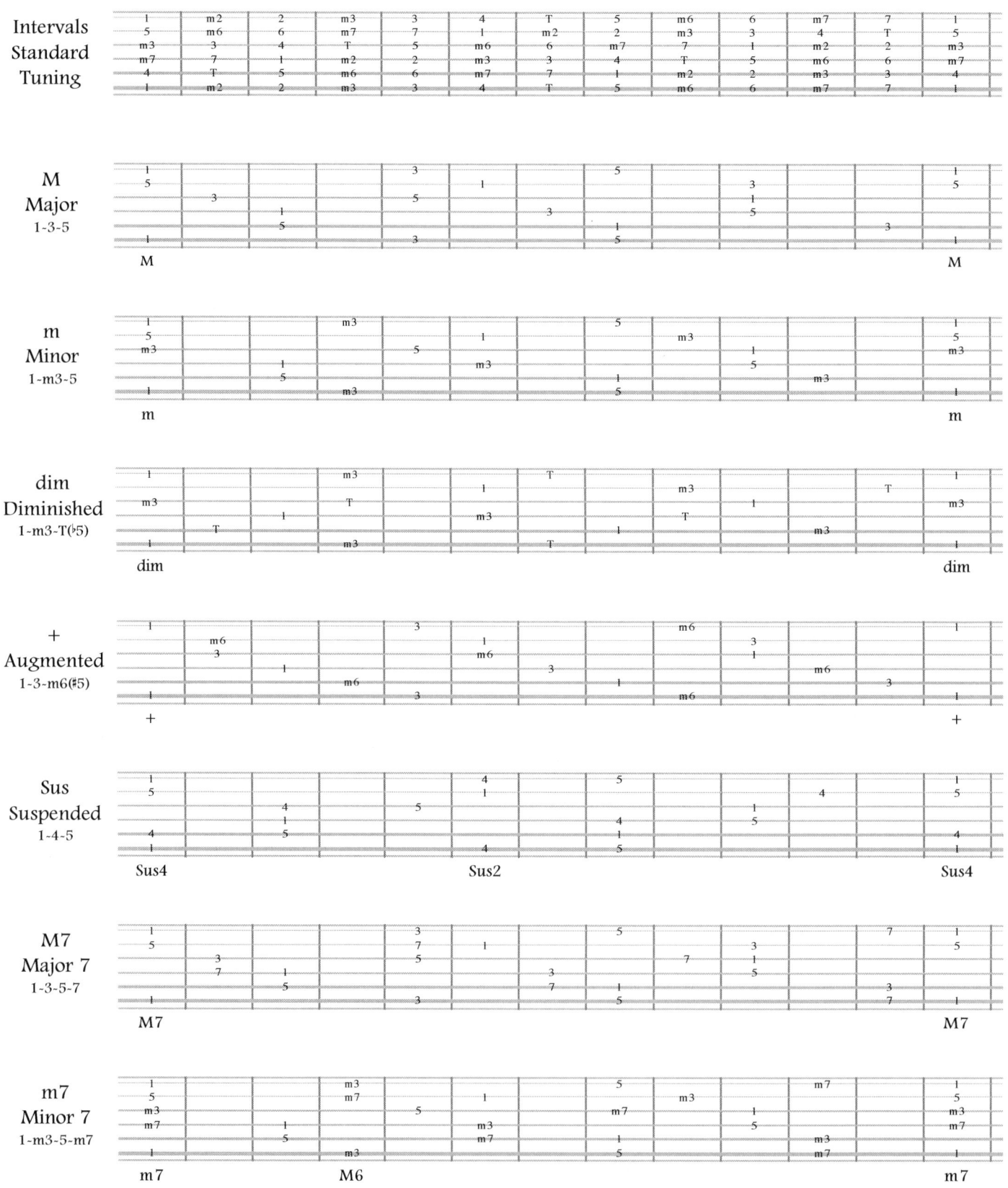

COMMON CHORD TYPES ~ FRETBOARD MAPS
For Standard Tuning(1~4~m7~m3~5~1)

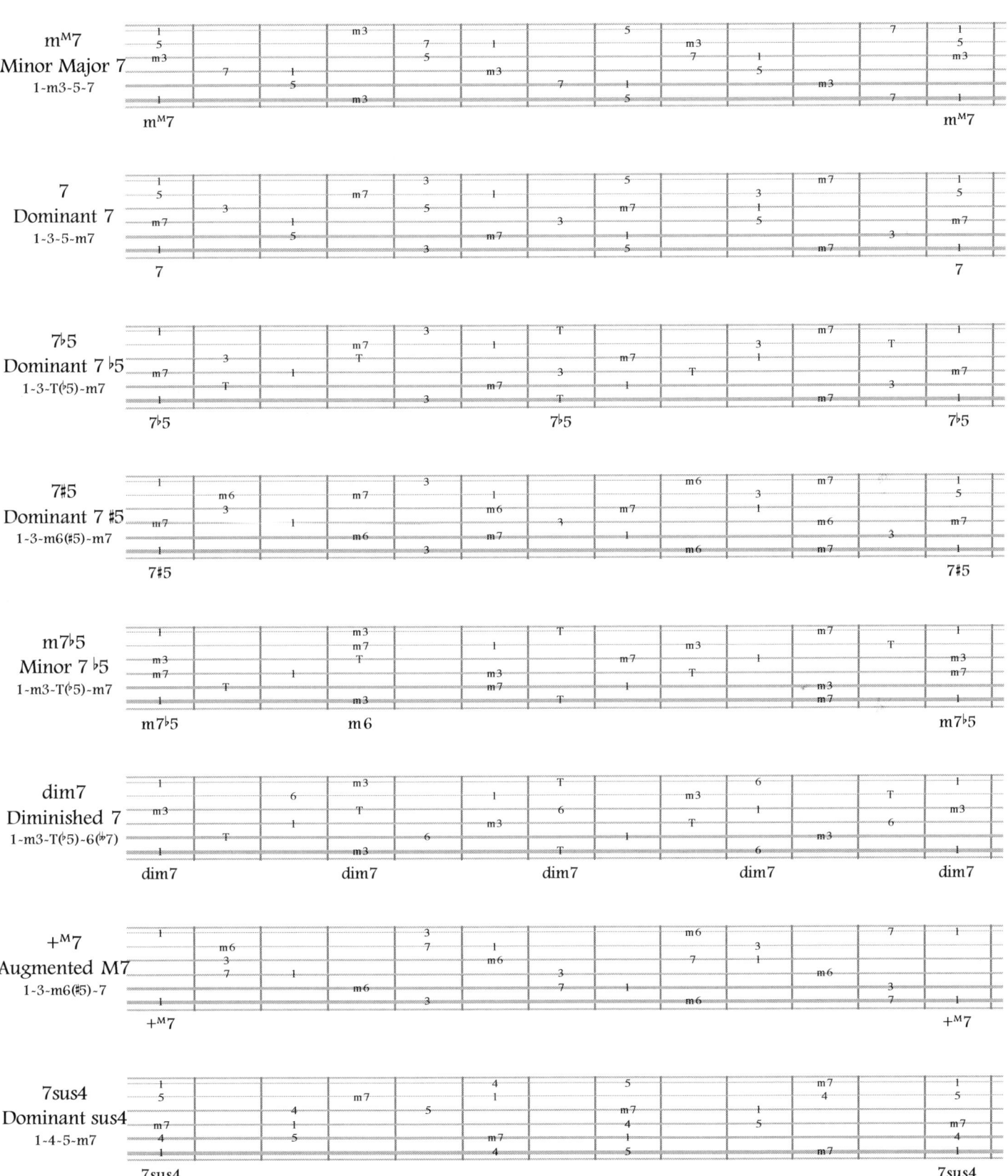

INDEX OF TRADITIONAL SCALE NAMES

Kanthamani Mela (2~3~T~5~m6~6) !3/4   Sarasangi Mela (2~3~4~5~m6~7) 5/1
Karaharapriya Mela (2~m3~4~5~6~m7) 1/2   Senavathi Mela (m2~m3~4~5~m6~6) 4/3
Kiravani Mela (2~m3~4~5~m6~7) 6/1   Shadhvidha Margini Mela (m2~m3~T~5~6~m7) 10/1
Kokilapriya Mela (m2~m3~4~5~6~7) 3/1   Shanmukapriya Mela (2~m3~T~5~m6~m7) 7/4
Kosalam Mela (m3~3~T~5~6~7) 6/6   Shubhapanthuvarali Mela (m2~m3~T~5~m6~7) 12/1
Lathangi Mela (2~3~T~5~m6~7) 4/4   Shulini Mela (m3~3~4~5~6~7) 7/6
Manavathi Mela (m2~2~4~5~6~7) !3/1   Shyamalangi Mela (2~m3~T~5~m6~6) !1/4
Mararanjani Mela (2~3~4~5~m6~6) !2/4   Simhendra Madhyamam Mela (2~m3~T~5~m6~7) 8/4
Mayamalava Gowla Mela (m2~3~4~5~m6~7) 8/1   Sucharithra Mela (m3~3~T~5~m6~6) !19/1
Mechakalyani Mela (2~3~T~5~6~7) 1/4   Suryakantam Mela (m2~3~4~5~6~7) 4/1
Naganandhini Mela (2~3~4~5~m7~7) 11/6   Suvarnangi Mela (m2~m3~T~5~6~7) 9/1
Namanarayani Mela (m2~3~T~5~m6~m7) 15/1   Thanarupi Mela (m2~2~4~5~m7~7) !4/1
Nasika Bhushani Mela (m3~3~T~5~6~m7) 10/3   Vachaspathi Mela (2~3~T~5~6~m7) 2/4
Natakapriya Mela (m2~m3~4~5~6~m7) 2/2   Vagadhisvari Mela (m3~3~4~5~6~m7) 11/3
Natabhairavi Mela (2~m3~4~5~m6~m7) 1/6   Vakulabharanam Mela (m2~3~4~5~m6~m7) 6/5
Navanitham Mela (m2~2~T~5~6~m7) !14/1   Vanaspathi Mela (m2~2~4~5~6~m7) !2/1
Nithimathi Mela (2~m3~T~5~m7~7) !10/4   Varunapriya Mela (2~m3~4~5~m7~7) !8/1
Pavani Mela (m2~2~T~5~6~7) !15/1   Vishvambhari Mela (m2~3~T~5~m7~7) !1/2
Ragavardhani Mela (m3~3~4~5~m6~m7) !8/5   Yagapriya Mela (m3~3~4~5~m6~6) !9/1
Ragupriya Mela (m2~2~T~5~m7~7) !16/1   **JAPANESE**
Ramapriya Mela (m2~3~T~5~6~m7) 14/1   Hirojoshi (2~m3~5~m6) 5 tones
Rasikapriya Mela (m3~3~T~5~m7~7) 8/2   In (m2~m3~4~5~m6~m7) 1/3
Rathnangi Mela (m2~2~4~5~m6~m7) 13/7   Kumoi (m2~4~5~m6) 5 tones
Rishabhapriya Mela (2~3~T~5~m6~m7) 3/4   Nohkan (2~4~T~m6~6~7) 10/2
Rupavathi Mela (m2~m3~4~5~m7~7) !5/1   Ritsu (2~m3~4~5~6~m7) 1/2
Salagam Mela (m2~2~T~5~m6~6) !11/1   Ryo (2~3~T~5~6~7) 1/4

PITCH INTONATION - MICROTONES

Although the 12-tone system is sufficient to describe most basic scale forms, many traditional scales would only be considered to be played properly by varying the tuning slightly of our twelve EQUALLY SPACED tones. To measure these variations we use cents. The space between two half-steps is 100 cents, therefore we have 1200 cents to the octave. The chart on the next page shows two prominent microtonal systems next to our 12-tone equal temperament.

JUST INTONATION is a system where all tones relate to the tonic note by simple ratios that create the purest harmonies. For example, the interval nearly equivalent to our Perfect 5th (500 cents) is the ratio 3/2 (702 cents). Meaning that the tone vibrates 3 times for every 2 vibrations of the tonic. East Indian music is based on Just Intonation although they do not use all the tones presented here. The limitation of this system is that when you modulate, the notes are no longer in tune with the tonic, so each key has varying degrees of "in-tuneness".

The PYTHAGOREAN system uses the just 5th (702 cents), but derives all the other notes of the scale by stacking these 5ths. This creates more consistency between different keys, but less pure intervals in general. The Pythagorean tuning is prominent in the Middle East. The full system shown here, with 53 nearly equally spaced tones, is the basis of Turkish Classical music. This system is where we find the famous middle eastern "quarter-tones". Although this has evolved into a theoretically 24-tone equal tempered system. The original tones were derived from the Pythagorean tuning and are usually closer to 40 cents flat than the 50 cents of an *equal quarter-tone*. Here are a few traditional quarter-tone scales of Arabic Classical music. I have used a "q" to indicate a tone a quarter-step lower than our standard interval:

Bastanikar (q2~q3~4~q5~qm6~q7~q8!(no octave!)   Nahfat (q2~m3~4~5~6~m7)
Bayatayn (q2~m3~4~q5~m6~m7)   Nairuz (2~q3~4~5~q6~m7)
Bayati (q2~m3~4~5~m6~m7)   Rast (Accending) (2~q3~4~5~6~q7)
Bayati Shuri (q2~m3~4~T~6~m7)   Rast (Descending) (2~q3~4~5~6~m7)
Hijaz (Accending) (m2~3~4~5~q6~m7)   Saba (q2~m3~3~5~m6~m7)
Husseini (q2~m3~4~5~q6~m7)   Sikah (Accending) (q2~q3~qT~5~q6~q7)
Huzam (q2~q3~q4~qm6~q6~q7)   Sikah (Descending) (q2~q3~qT~q5~q6~q7)
Iraq (q2~q3~4~q5~q6~q7)   Sikah Baladi (q2~q3~4~q5~q6~q7)
Mahur (2~q3~4~5~6~7)   Suznak (2~q3~4~5~m6~7)
Mustaar (qm3~q3~qT~q5~q6~q7)   Ushaq Masri (2~m3~4~5~q6~m7)

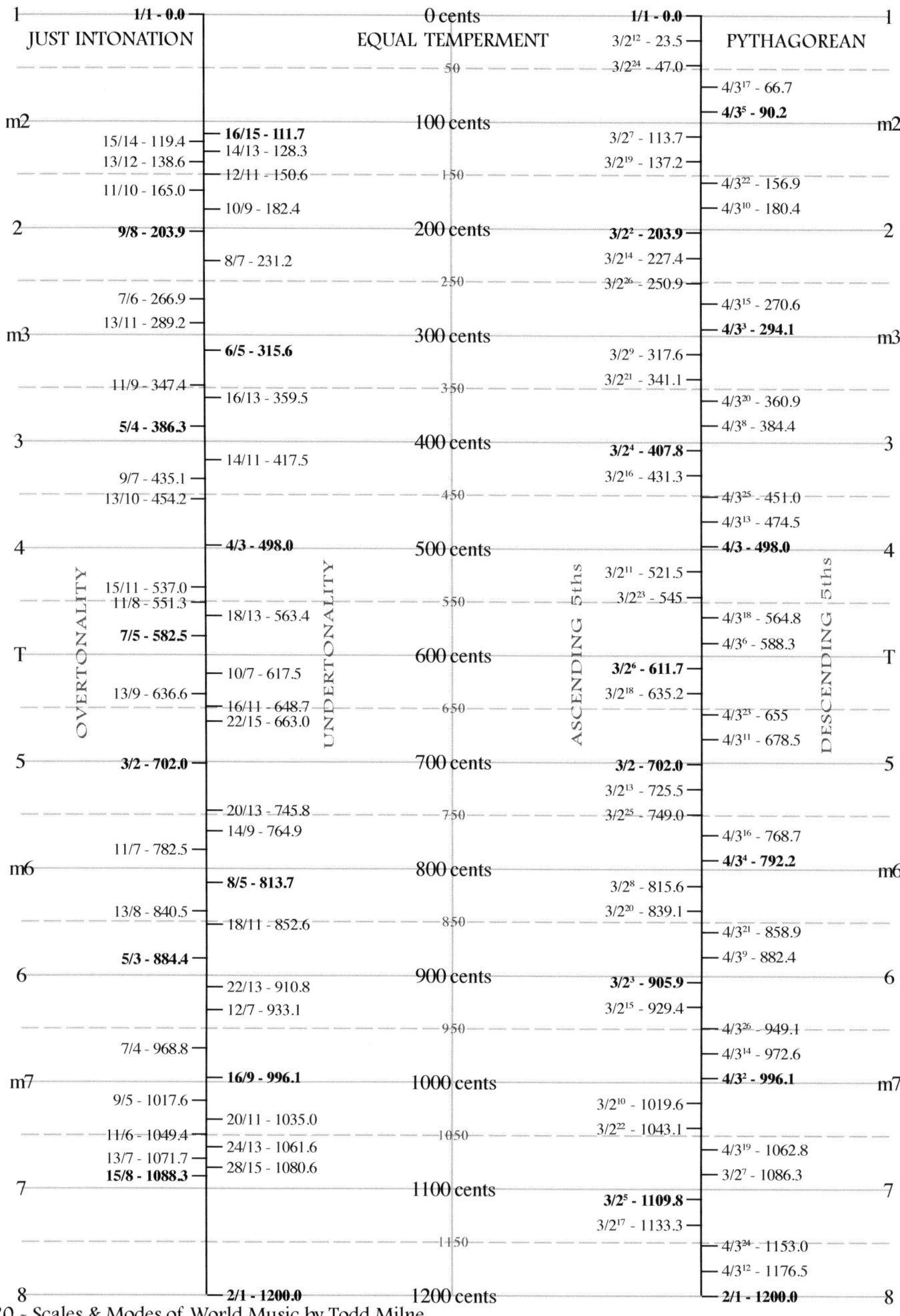

The point in dealing with all this theory is to make better music. In cataloging all these scales and modes, I was not intending to just show you 252 ways to move your fingers. Each interval possesses its own "emotional" characteristic. And each scale is a combination of these expressive musical colors with the ability to create a mood all it's own. In order to really use these scales you have to really hear them. Then they become tools you use to express yourself. Understanding and cultivating the emotive nature of sound is what it means to be a musician.

One of the best ways I've found to bring out the sound of the different scales & modes is to play them over a sustained drone on the tonic note. This emphasizes the harmonic colors more than just playing the notes in succession with no accompaniment. Sound files for this book can be found at MilneSounds.com/Scales. I start with a lesson to explain how this works, followed by twelve drone tracks tuned to the notes of the chromatic scale. Enjoy!

About the Author: Todd Milne is the owner and head producer of Perimeter Sound Arts, a music production and sound design studio for software applications, television, internet and other media. He holds a degree in Commercial Music/Jazz Studies and a certificate in Music Technology. Mr. Milne has studied, performed and recorded music for over 25 years, undertaking studies in sound physics, instrument design, esoteric music theory and many conventional approaches and practices, as well as incorporating methods spanning the musical spectrum of the worlds cultures. His work always brings an element of innovation and fusion of diverse influences. "My goal as an educator is to bring together new musical resources and make them more accessible to all musicians."

MilneSounds.com

Made in the USA
Las Vegas, NV
08 August 2024

93493731R00015